CW01083782

VOLLEYBALL:
TECHNIQUES AND TACTICS

TONI FAOUZI TAHTOUH (PH.D)

Copyright © 2017 Toni Faouzi Tahtouh (Ph.D).

All rights reserved. No part of this book may be reproduced, stored, or transmitted by any means—whether auditory, graphic, mechanical, or electronic—without written permission of both publisher and author, except in the case of brief excerpts used in critical articles and reviews. Unauthorized reproduction of any part of this work is illegal and is punishable by law.

ISBN: 978-1-4834-7267-6 (sc)
ISBN: 978-1-4834-7266-9 (hc)
ISBN: 978-1-4834-7268-3 (e)

Because of the dynamic nature of the Internet, any web addresses or links contained in this book may have changed since publication and may no longer be valid. The views expressed in this work are solely those of the author and do not necessarily reflect the views of the publisher, and the publisher hereby disclaims any responsibility for them.

Any people depicted in stock imagery provided by Thinkstock are models, and such images are being used for illustrative purposes only.
Certain stock imagery © Thinkstock.

Lulu Publishing Services rev. date: 08/14/2017

Acknowledgment and Dedication

I would like to dedicate this book to every sportsman and sportswoman, to sports fans in general and volleyball fans in particular and last but not least to trainers, coaches and players of this beautiful sport.

I take this opportunity to thank each and every person that helped making this book a success. I thank my late father Faouzi Ibrahim Tahtouh and my mother Sayde Abou Assaf Tahtouh (may God prolong her life) for their patience and tolerance throughout the years. I would like to thank as well my brothers Nicolas, Boulos, Boutros, Maroun, Joseph, Salah and George Tahtouh as well as my sister Antoinette Tahtouh Chamoun and her husband the lawyer Joseph Wadih Chamoun. Another thank you goes to my loving and encouraging cousin the lawyer Michel Abou Hanna and my brother in law Elie Jeries Kallas who executed the illustrations on this book. Special thank you goes to my wife Joumana and my precious kids from whom I had to be away sometimes during the preparation of this book, and to each and every person who contributed, from close or far, to the execution of this book.

Toni Faouzi Tahtouh (Ph.D)

Introduction

DEFINITION OF VOLLEYBALL

The sport of volleyball, regardless of its novelty, is considered one of the most popular sports practiced by kids and adults, and in which excel male and female players in a collective coordination.

This sport becomes even more spectacular when the players show a great deal of techniques and skills. Besides their skills, players have to go the extra mile in order to respond to the circumstances of the collective game, and this is where the beauty of team work lies.

Once again, this confirms that volleyball is a team sport that works in a harmonious and coordinated way just like an orchestra, where each musician is an entity by himself yet so integrated in the group that it looks like one person delivering an excellent performance.

In the course of this book, we will be discussing the origins and basis of indoor and outdoor volleyball, also known as beach or sand volleyball. We will be discussing as well the current rules and regulations, which tend to be modified by the experts almost after each Olympic Games or International Championship.

All the subjects discussed in this book have been studied in a profound, objective and scientific way by focusing on the main technical and tactical factors and analyzing the different methods that help improve and develop this sport. In the first place, the focus was given to the importance of preparation and training of junior players who are considered the foundation of any strong and skilled team capable of progressing and excelling in this sport.

Perhaps it is the extensive experience that I gained by practicing volleyball in different places in the world, such as Lebanon, Europe, and the former Soviet Union and the United States that has empowered me to fully capture the aspects of this sport's organization, planning and training. It has also given me the drive and knowledge to discuss these aspects in a detailed yet simplified educational way, giving coaches and players the opportunity to apply this information in their teams in order to maximize both preparation and results.

It goes without saying that the lack of similar studies in our libraries has motivated me to write this book using for reference the most scientific sports compilation and my personal experience from studying and practicing this sport for a long time.

I hope that my book will make a difference in the future of volleyball, and I look forward to subsequent studies in this field that will help improve, develop and advance this sport.

Toni Faouzi Tahtouh (Ph.D)

CONTENTS

PART ONE

ORIGINS OF VOLLEYBALL

Chapter One

HISTORY OF VOLLEYBALL

Volleyball originated in the United States and had its first rules established in 1895. In the early days, it used to be practiced without any prior training, and in July 1896 was given the name of **volleyball**. In 1897, the rules were modified and applied all over the United States. These rules had 10 stipulations, of which we mention the most important:

- Size of the court 7.6 m x 15.1 m [25 ft. x 50 ft.]

- Height of the net 1.98 m [6.5 ft.]

- The ball is made of leather or synthetic leather filled with air and has a circumference of 63.5 – 68.5 cm [2 – 2.3 ft.] and weighs 340 g [0.765 lbs.].

- For serve, the player stands on one leg on the back row and hits the ball with an open hand. In case of a serving error, a second try is allowed.

- It is considered a fault when the ball touches the net during the game.

- The number of players participating in the game is not specified.

- It is considered a fault when the ball falls on the line marking the boundaries of the court.

- The winning point is only given to the serving team if he wins the rally.

Volleyball was quickly spreading all over the Unites States and gaining popularity year after year, as it was practiced on all social and academic levels. Soon afterwards, it spread throughout the world and was being played equally by professionals and amateurs.

In 1922 Brooklyn city held its first official volleyball game, and in the same year the United States requested that volleyball be included in 8th Olympic Games held in Paris in 1924.

Since volleyball became popular on a global scale, some rules were modified as follows:

- In 1912 court's dimensions set at 10.6 m x 18.2 m [35 ft. x 60 ft.], height of the net at 2.28 m [7.5 ft.] and width at 91 cm [3 ft.]. Change of player when serve is lost.

- In 1917 the height of the net set at 2.43 m [8 ft.] as well as the rule of 15 points per set.

- In 1918 the number of players per team set at six.

- In 1921 a line was introduced in the middle of the court under the net.

- In 1922 the rule of three hits per side was adopted.

- In 1923 the court's dimensions reduced to 9 m x 18 m [29.7 ft. x 59.4 ft.].

The game witnessed major changes, technically and tactically, between 1929 and 1939 when the collective block was introduced, making the spike stronger and more controlled. The lateral spike was introduced to escape the block and setting was being done with more sophistication.

In Berlin's conference, during the 11th Olympic Games in the German capital in 1936, Ravitch Maslowtski was elected 1st president of the committee that was composed of 13 European countries, 5 American countries and 4 Asian countries.

The committee adopted the American rules as general rules for this game after making some changes of which we mention the most important:

- The ball can be played with any part of the body above the waist.

- The height of the net for female players set at 2.24 m [7.4 ft.].

- The serve has to be done from behind the back line.

The committee tried to include the sport in the Olympic Games held in Japan in 1940.

In April 1947, after the end of the Second World War, 14 countries participated in the first international conference for volleyball. The conference decided to found the International Federation for Volleyball (FIVB) who worked hard to control, develop and regulate this game.

After that, the FIVB went on organizing the European championship, the world championship and the European championship cup. The first World championship was organized in 1949 for men and 1952 for women. The next important date was1964 when volleyball was included in the Olympic Games in Tokyo.

In 1994 in Athens, the FIVB once again modified some of the rules by allowing the ball to touch any part of the body including the feet on condition that it happens in one go during handling the ball. It allowed as well the serve to be received with the fingers for setting compared to before where it had to be received from below.

In 1998 during a press conference in Tokyo, Dr. Robin Acosta the president of the FIVB announced some new changes to the rules to be applied during the world championship in Japan and here are some of these modifications:

- Each team can choose from a final list of 12 players, one "libero" to participate in the whole championship and his role is to defend from the back row. Specific rules were set for this player with regards to defending and receiving from the back row. He was not allowed to pursue the attack when the ball is at the top of the net. The "libero" has to wear a distinctive colored shirt and can't be substituted.

- The coach can move and stand up during the rally. Cheering from the rest of the players sitting on the bench in the warming zone is allowed without causing disturbance or delay to the game.

- The ball has to be spherical made of leather or synthetic leather of different light colors according to the guidelines of FIVB.

- The uniforms have to be comfortable yet not too baggy. Long sleeves are not allowed. Numbers can only be on the short's right leg, country's flag and name on the front of the shirt. The surname or nickname on the back. Women are allowed to wear one piece kits.

Upon the request of the Federation's board, 174 countries unanimously agreed in Tokyo to modify the scoring system as follows:

- The team scores a point even if it wasn't serving.

- 25 point rally system with an advantage not exceeding 2 points (for example 25 - 23). In case of tie break (24 – 24), the game will continue until one team wins by 2 points (26 – 24) or (27 – 25) for example. If there is a tie break in sets 2 - 2 then the last set will go to 15 points and the winner is the one who gets the first two point advantage.

- Serve ball can touch the top of the net and cross it.

In 2012 in Anaheim an edition has been commissioned by the 33rd FIVB world congress new changes to the rules to be applied during the games between 2013 and 2016. Here are some of these modifications:

- A team may consist of up to 12 players, one coach, and a maximum of two assistant coaches, one team therapist and one medical doctor.

- It is a fault, during the reception of serve, to make a double contact or catch using an overhand finger action.

- If the libero is expelled or disqualified, he/she may be replaced immediately by the team's second libero. Should the team have only one libero, then it has the right to make a re-designation.

In the Rio Olympic Games 2016 in Brazil, the video challenge system helps officials and players see the net faults, block touches, ball into antenna, line calls and foot faults clearly.

FIVB president Dr. Ary S. Graça said: "The FIVB is focused on improving the resources available to referees to ensure the game is absolutely fair to the athlete's actions. The volleyball challenge system is a great example of such an improvement."

The 2017-2020 Official Volleyball and Official Beach Volleyball Rules don't include any major changes to the current rules that were agreed on at the 35th FIVB world congress. The rules became effective in competition on January 1st, 2017.

Volleyball became the most popular sport and was played on a large scale in sport clubs and schools. The ongoing development of this sport led to the strict application of rules by the referees, especially when it came to counting faults as little as they may be. This made the players carefully prepare for their attack hits before executing them. Spiking from the first set was rarely used in order to guarantee a successful hit and avoid inefficiency. Blockers were now allowed to reach beyond the net when blocking. Due to this new rule the attacking team had to adopt specific tactics to overcome the opponent's defense strategy. At the same time, the serve became faster and lower.

The changes to the rules never really stopped. Many have been made until now and are still being made.

This quick review of the history and development gives us an idea about the authenticity of this sport and its interaction in different countries and on different levels which puts it ahead of other sports and makes it the youth favorite game.

Chapter Two

General Characteristics

Volleyball is a sport played by two teams on a playing court divided by a net.

Court's dimensions: 18 m [59.4 ft.] length and 9 m [29.7 ft.] width including the 3 m [9.9 ft.] line from the net known as the attack line. The axis of the center line divides the playing court into 2 equal courts measuring 9 m x 9 m [29.7 ft. x 29.7 ft.] each. The entire width of the line is considered to belong to both courts equally. This line extends beneath the net from side to side line.

All the lines in the court should be 5 cm [0.165 ft.] wide.

Net's height: 2.43 m [8 ft.] for men and 2.24 m [7.4 ft.] for women.

Net's height varies according to categories and age.

Ages	Males	Females
45 years and above	2.38 m [7.85 ft.]	2.19 m [7.23 ft.]
44 to 15 years	2.43 m [8 ft.]	2.24 m [7.4 ft.]
14 and 13 years	2.24 m [7.4 ft.]	2.24 m [7.4 ft.]
12 and 11 years	2.13 m [7 ft.]	2.13 m [7 ft.]
10 years and below	2.13 m [7 ft.]	1.98 m [6.53 ft.]

The ball: circumference between 65 cm [2.14 ft.] and 67 cm [2.21 ft.].

Weight: between 260 g [0.6 lbs.] and 280 g [0.63 lbs.].

World and official competitions, as well as national or league championship, must be played with FIVB approved balls, unless by agreement of FIVB.

PART TWO

PREPARATORY
STRATEGIES

Chapter Three

PREPARATORY STRATEGIES

Volleyball players are gradually prepared through a learning process and an adjustable training. The coach has to have in place an adjustable strategy that suits the capacity of his team in order for the training to be effective and to take its natural and correct course.

Chapter Four

CONCEPT OF STRATEGY

In order to achieve the desired goal, the strategy requires the presence of various connected elements which means from a practical point of view one specific strategy with united elements. The fundamental general strategy starts in the early preparation of young talents between the age of 8 and 10 in order to produce a successful and competent team, who is capable, both physically and technically, of achieving excellent results. This preparation goes up to 19 years old.

The preparation of an Olympic team can only take place after around four years of ongoing work and training, both theoretical and technical. The players should have a high fitness level achieved through an extensive physical and psychological training.

The national coach chooses the players of the Olympic team from amongst the best and promising players in the national teams.

The coaches have to coordinate their strategies according to the needs of each team.

They may have in place many strategies that complement each other in order to cover all the needs of the different teams and to help form a national team from the elite players already trained in the preliminary or excellent teams.

On the other hand, each coach has his own special strategy that contributes positively to the progress of the team.

Chapter Five

STRATEGY SETTING

The strategy is composed of different channels and forms a connected network regardless of the different elements. Taking into consideration those high results can't be achieved starting from a non-homogenous or weak situation, the strategy aims at forming a general status for the team by developing its qualities and capacities through ongoing training. It is a fact that a team can't reach high levels when its organizational development is neither sound nor scientific regardless of its nature.

Chapter Six

PREPARATORY ORGANIZATION

Whether the goal is to have a first class team or an Olympic one, the preparatory organization starts from the very beginning.

Specialized coaches will choose good players between the age of 11 and 13 years old. They will work on developing their capacities through certain tools as well as positively help shape their progress and development so they can reach high levels which will allow some of them to become part of the national team.

Chapter Seven

LEARNING - TRAINING PROCESS

The process of training and preparation means a lot for the chosen elements of the team. At the beginning, the focus should be given to the quality of these elements, their development, progress, capacities and assimilation of specific strategies.

The correct and scientific approach to the learning progress on its own will give successful and guaranteed results.

On the practical front, the focus should be given to the games and drills which complement the basic training, provided that the coach draws a conclusion regarding the level of progress reached by these elements in a specific period of time. During the preparatory progress a detailed exercise and games calendar should be used, and the players should follow a specific and appropriate lifestyle suitable for their activities.

PART THREE

PREPARATION OF THE PLAYERS

Chapter Eight

PREPARATION OF
THE PLAYERS

Taking into consideration that player's capacity reaches its best between the age of 24 and 28 years for men and between 22 and 26 for women, and in order to get good results from the preparation, players between the age of 9 and 30 years old should follow regular and ongoing training. Some experienced players may continue in this sport for longer, particularly skillful setters who are the brain and engine of the team and hold a key position for the success of the strategy and the achievement of the attack.

The reason that setters have a longer career is because they spend more time mastering the required skills, from sharpness of mind to flexibility and wisdom, in order to become a successful setter and a positive factor on the team.

Training is done according to age, where the training for boys and girls between the age of 10 and 13 for example have to be stimulating and consisting of light practical exercises to prevent any damage to their health.

Chapter Nine

PLAYERS' BASIC DUTIES

In order to gain experience and fitness level as well as acquire the necessary skills to reach high and guaranteed goals, players have to listen to their coach, follow his instructions and strategies and execute the given exercises with sportsmanship and persistence.

Chapter Ten

ETHICS AND CONDUCT

Volleyball is a team sport that requires sacrifice and perseverance in order to produce results; therefore, players have to have a high level of sportsmanship and ethics. The more duties and ethics are respected, the more the training and competitions become successful and productive.

One of the various goals of training is to strengthen players' physical fitness as well as other skills such as: strength, speed, endurance, agility, smartness and flexibility. Mastering the important movements in various activities such as walking, running, jumping, throwing and swimming, help improve the general health and fitness level on one hand and strengthen the organs and muscles that do most of the work during the games on the other hand. Moreover, these skills help master the techniques more rapidly and ensure the success of the strategies.

Players have to effectively master the attack and defense tactics both individually and collectively.

The more the players master the techniques the easier it is for them to execute the strategies during the games.

The coach has to eliminate the tendency to individualism and prepare them to play as a team in a harmonious and consistent environment, by collaborating amongst each other during the training and the games.

By gaining theoretical and practical knowledge of the strategy and its details, success becomes more achievable.

Moreover, by gaining expertise from the repetitive training and games, the players develop their connection with each other and become more homogenous, which gives them a better chance at reaching their goals.

Volleyball players should strengthen their nervous system through training in order to prevent tension which is considered the first cause for loss and lack of collective work. Injuries can be prevented as well through the right preparation.

In order for the preparation to be complete and effective, it should include all the duties mentioned above.

Chapter Eleven

METHODS USED
IN TRAINING

Executed during and after preparation, these training movements give the players basic experience through developing and strengthening their organs to perform specific skills such as receiving the ball. They are used as well to develop the kinetic characteristics and biological skills.

To avoid injuries, players have to warm up before the start of the game.

During competitions, the coach has to use a didactic calendar. He needs to put the team through specific exercises to develop their attack and defense techniques, as well as the required tactics for the game.

The completion of a strategy requires from the coach serious work on a scientific level. He has to be capable of providing his team, during training and competitions on both practical and psychological levels, with knowledge and care. In this sense, he may shorten or extend the break for example, in order to achieve the desired result.

PART FOUR

TECHNIQUES

Chapter Twelve

TECHNICAL PREPARATION

The success of volleyball players depends a lot of the times on the level of their techniques and their mastering of this art. Technique itself is knowing how to execute the basic skills in the best way and avoiding mistakes through a preparatory and progressive program. After the ready position for example, the player has to react with the ball either to receive it or to attack by jumping and hitting it in a coordinated movement. The whole operation can be reduced to specific moves from serving to receiving, setting, spiking and blocking.

The preparatory period of the technique is very important and should be done step by step with the beginners. If we consider that the technique is the base of volleyball and the stronger the base is the better the outcome will be, then, the more the beginners master the hands and feet movement and how to position themselves in the right way, the easier it will be for them to progress in this sport.

It goes without saying that the more the players master the techniques the faster and stronger their progress will be. To start with, beginners should have the required fitness level and desire to learn this beautiful game, and then the coach polishes and develops these attributes through training.

The rules of the game, such as not allowing the ball to touch the ground, the technical factors as well as the scoring system and counting errors are what make volleyball distinctive. In order to fulfill their basic duties efficiently and skillfully, volleyball players need to have excellent physical strength and high level of sportsmanship.

Chapter Thirteen

SPECIFIC CHARACTERISTICS

Volleyball players need to have specific characteristics regarding weight and size. Furthermore, if we consider that the human body works according to the lever system then surely having long limbs would be a positive attribute.

The rules of the game require the use of both arms in performing most of the movements. For this reason, these parts require specific characteristics in order to express the relation between the form and the function. The repetitive use of these parts in a specific direction leads to changes in their physical shape, which allows a better performance and a natural progress within a measured scientific methodology.

Chapter Fourteen

TECHNICAL PREPARATION FOR THE BASIC SKILLS

Without explaining the purpose for it, the coach asks the players to do exercises that are technically difficult such as spiking with the ball hanging or held in the air, or blocking with both palm heels as well as receiving the ball in easy and difficult situations. Afterwards, the coach points out the errors so that the players are able to optimally perform these duties next time. What is important during training is the direction of the work; regardless of the difference in technique between one player and another due to one's own style and method.

During training and the learning process, the focus should be given to the duty of receiving, how to technically execute it as well as the right place and position for it. On this basis, a high level of interaction can be reached between the players during attack and defense.

The coach works on strengthening the player's physical capacities, especially the fundamental muscle group, as well as developing the collective experience such as: blocking, preparing to receive, spiking, the vertical jump, the rhythm, moving three steps, end of movement, hitting the ball, blocking with one or more players, setting to any direction and moving quickly to receive the ball or block it. The coach gives the players technical and tactical drills, as well as physical exercises to strengthen their muscles and joints in order to avoid injuries and perform the defense and attack duties in the best way.

PART FIVE

TACTICS

Chapter Fifteen

TACTICAL PREPARATION

Once the volleyball player has mastered the right movement and position for the required skills, the focus is given then to developing his alertness, capacity to fill the court and how to move in a harmonious and interactive way with the other players during defense and attack.

When applying the attack strategies, it is important to read the movement of the opposition. On this basis, the coach will choose what strategy to use by pointing out the opponents' weaknesses in order to achieve a win. During the game, when the ball is moving backwards and forwards between the two teams, each player is considered an important factor. Therefore, players must be able to work in harmony within the team on an individual, dual and collective level in order to execute the specific duties during attack and defense.

Chapter Sixteen

CONCEPT OF COLLECTIVE TACTICS

The collective tactic is collaboration between two or more players to achieve a certain move for the team. The interaction between these players doesn't only specify touching the ball three times, but also specifies from where to perform a spike.

Almost in all cases, after receiving the ball from the serve or the attack, the ball should be directed to the setter who will be either in the attack line or moving up from the defense line. The players have to be ready at all times to spike either from the first or the second set and from any zone in a coordinated way depending on the situation and conditions of the game. All these elements are considered a collective coordination originating from a specific tactical harmony between the players. In order for this harmony to be successful, players should know how and where to set for a spike as well as how to receive the ball and redirect it to the required zone.

When setting the ball, the setter has to be aware of the gaps in the opponent's team or their blocking weaknesses, and accordingly direct the ball to the right attacker on his team giving him the power to spike with the least amount of confrontation with the opposition. The setter who is moving from the back row has to avoid receiving the ball. His mission at this time consists in moving to the attack line without causing any disturbance to the player closer to him.

If the setter has to receive the ball, then the setter should set it directly to the attacker. If the attacker sees that the ball will be blocked, the attacker should set the ball to a second player in order to do this task. The team should be certain of the zone where the setter is moving to. However, if the serve is directed at the setter then the setter should choose a better zone to move to.

The attacker should be ready at all times to perform all kinds of spikes depending on the conditions of the game and the coach's instructions. This means that the attacker can spike or drop the ball in an empty spot in the opponent's court if he was faced with a roof block whether the set was short, fast, snatched or vertical. If there are three attackers, then it's essential that they move when the setter moves up from the defense line. In the case that there are two attackers and the ball is set from a player in the attack line, then they should move to the net as if they are all hitting the ball in order to deceive the opponents and weaken their block.

For great results, the tactical methods should be coordinated and fully executed in the right position without delay. The understanding that players have amongst each other, whether in words or hand signals, helps them fulfill their duties and conceal the opposition when it comes to setting or directing the ball. Success comes when they commit to translate their knowledge into actions, as in this example:

- Attackers coordinating amongst each other: attacker of zone 3 moves quickly to jump and spike when the ball is in the air swerving to the right in his zone. Shortly after, player of zone 2 moves quickly to zone 3 crossing player of zone 3 and jumping to his left, then player of zone 4 moves forward quickly to hit the long, fast or half long set to the edge of the net. (Picture 16-1)

Picture 16-1 Player of zone 3 moves first

Chapter Seventeen

TACTICAL ATTACK

The interaction amongst the players of one team during attack is the only guarantee to achieve a successful outcome.

The more the attack line players participate in the attack, the better it will be and the harder for the opponents to block. When an attack line player makes a set, the team will automatically lose an attacker and will end up with two instead of three which makes it easier for the opponents to guess the direction of the ball and easier for them to block it. The team will have superiority and advantage if its technical and tactical level is high when it comes to overcoming the opponents block. In some cases, the strategy changes according to the situation, where one player might stand by the net and the attack becomes the responsibility of the strongest attackers on the attack line, for example:

- The player making the second setting stands in zone 2. The two players of zones 4 and 3 are in attack and the first set goes to zone 2. The attacker in zone 3 moves automatically to attack from a low set in his zone behind the setter who sees that the hit will be collectively blocked, then at the last minute sets the ball to an attacker in zone 4 who spikes or drops the ball in an empty spot which depends on the attacker and his capacity to think wisely and execute successfully. (Pictures 17-1 and 2)

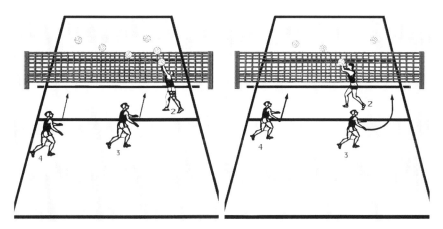

Picture 17-1   Picture 17-2

A player moving from the defense line to make a second set gives the team the opportunity to apply different strategies. It is important that the team has three attackers, preferably well at setting.

The setter has to be ready at all time to move from the defense line and sets the ball to the attacker to spike.

Chapter Eighteen

STRATEGIES AND COORDINATION

When establishing a strategy, players have to get involved in its coordination and gradual execution in order to perform it with precision and proficiency. The setter has to agree with the rest of the players on specific signals to use during the game.

Hereafter are some strategies:

- If the received ball is directed from zone 5 to zone 3 and player of zone 6 moving up to set, then the two attackers of zone 4 and 2 have to immediately move forward to the center of the net to spike from a low set. In case the opponents make a collective block in the middle of the net, then the setter has to rapidly set the ball to zone 4 where player of zone 3 had automatically moved there to spike. (Picture 18-1)

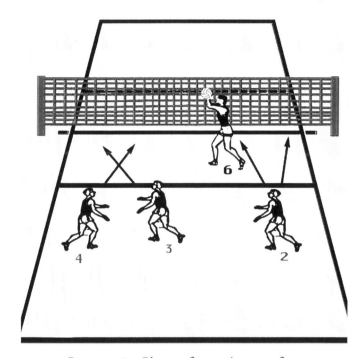

Picture 18-1 Player of zone 4 moves first

- If the received ball gets directed to zone 2 then player of zone 1 moves to make a second set, the attacker in zone 2 goes out fast to spike in zone 3, and the attacker in zone 3 goes out to spike in zone 2.

The setter bends forward slightly and signals that it will be a long set to the edge of the net, and without delay, sets the ball behind him to zone 2 where the player in zone 3 spikes instead. (Picture 18-2)

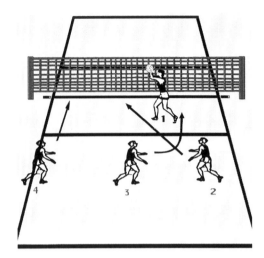

Picture 18-2 Player of zone 2 moves first

- The attack can be done as in the previous picture, but at the last minute the attacker of zone 3 swerves into zone 2. Player of zone 2 would have moved beforehand to zone 3 to spike, but instead the setter quickly directs the ball to the edge of the net in zone 4. (Picture 18-3)

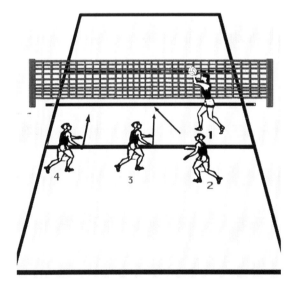

Picture 18-3 Player of zone 2 moves first

- The ball is directed to zone 4. Player of zone 5 moves to the 2nd set. In the meantime player of zone 3 moves quickly to zone 4. Player of zone 4 automatically moves to zone 3 and pretends to make an attack then the ball is rapidly set to the player in zone 2 who executes the strategy. (Picture 18-4)

Picture 18-4 Player of zone 3 moves first

The diversity of strategies that can be applied gives a fundamental picture to the coordination that is needed during the game. Furthermore, the tactical flexibility of a team lies in knowing when and how to switch strategies.

After the serve, it is recommendable that all players move forward or backward. It is also important that the reception of the ball is done by the defense line players that are not participating in the attack, keeping the skilled receiver in the most exposed zone.

PART SIX

FUNDAMENTAL SKILLS

Chapter Nineteen

SERVING

Serving is an individual technique executed from behind the inline, by hitting the ball one single hit. The server has to look to the opponent's court to identify the flight path of the ball.

When training for serving the focus should be on releasing or tossing the ball to the required height and repeating this operation until it becomes precise and confident. The higher and more correctly the ball is tossed the better the impact will be. The shoulder and hand should be solid and connected, and the palm hitting the ball should be tense at the wrist. In order to master the serve, the players have to repetitively practice it during training, focusing on the details from choosing the zone to hitting the ball in order to perform a precise, correct and effective serve.

Besides the traditional way to serve by hitting the ball hard while jumping, new methods have started to rely on the light long serve which is harder to receive and messes up the opponents strategies. Nevertheless, the focus during training should be on the strength and precision of the hit as well as its course. Players should focus as well on choosing the right direction and different distances for the serve, this way training their muscles to perform in all kinds of situations. It should be mentioned here that the style of serve currently used, which is jumping from behind the end line and hitting the ball while it's in the air, is very similar to a spike.

- **Underhand serves.** Where the player stands facing the net with one foot forward, the knees bent and the trunk slightly forward. The ball is placed on one hand which is bent at the wrist, so it can be tossed vertically. The hand is brought back previously or when releasing the ball in the air and the point of support moves according to the movement of the ball, from the right foot to the left foot or the other way around (Picture 19-1). The ball is hit with the hand moving from below to above and forward.

Picture 19-1

- **Lateral serves.** Is hitting the ball from underneath the shoulder level. The player stands laterally facing the net, leaning forward, bending the knee and pulling the shoulder backwards and downwards. After tossing the ball, it's hit at the waist level with the hand moving from the side. (Picture 19-2)

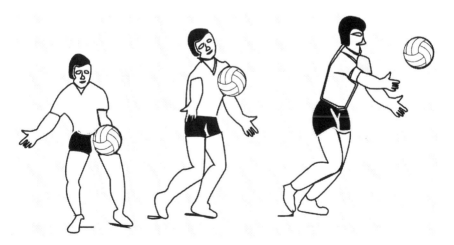

Picture 19-2

- **Floater or Drive serves.** The player stands facing the net and hits the ball from above the shoulder level. Both feet lined up about shoulder length apart with one foot forward. The ball is tossed up in the air then hit with the palm contacting the center of the ball. The hand should be stiff and open and the wrist should be straight.

Picture 19-3

As the player hits the ball, he sends all his weight from the arm to the ball. Then the point of support moves to the front foot as he steps forward once the ball is hit. (Picture 19-3)

- **Short serves.** The player pops the ball with a short follow-through to allow the ball to land in front of the attack line disrupting the hitters' tactic.

- **Lateral overhand serves.** Is done above the shoulder level by positioning the body laterally to the net. The player tosses the ball in the air above the head, and then leans the trunk backwards by lowering the shoulder and bending the knee. The player hits the ball with the palm. (Picture 19-4)

Picture 19-4

- **Jump serves**. Similar to a spike but done from the serve line. The ball is tossed high in the air, then the player makes a timed approach, jumps vertically swinging his arms, pushing the metatarsi and extending the knees and pelvis.

When jumping, the player places the hitting palm behind his shoulder and the elbow forward with the trunk slightly bent. The player hits the ball then lands on both metatarsi by bending the knees slightly to absorb the body weight.

The serve plays a key role in the game, especially if it's done correctly and is directed to the right zone. When serving the ball to the attack line on the opponent's court where the attackers stand, we hinder their attack strategy because these players are always ready to attack and not receive. The ball can also be directed between the players in the defense line or the sides which hinders the setter's movement, especially if the opposing team relies on him moving forward from there. A good strategy as well is to serve the ball in the middle between the attack line and the defense line, as this place is often empty. The ball can be directed as well to a specific player or according to the coach's instructions.

Some of the important factors for scoring points are the speed with which the strategies are executed, or the rhythm with which the players work together to prevent the other team from advancing. Another important detail during the game is substitutions as well as timeouts, where the coach can warn and guide the players, change a strategy and draw their attention to a weak zone in the opponent's team where they can serve and spike the ball to score easy points.

Players should keep their energy and enthusiasm high at all times during the games. They need to execute their duties to the full and keep a positive attitude amongst each other.

Chapter Twenty

SETTING

Setting is one of the basic skills that volleyball players need to master and execute during the game, in this category we find:

- The **low position** to cover the game and to start the attack.

- The **middle position** when preparing to set.

- The **defense position** to receive from below.

When taking the **low position**, both feet are parallel with one foot forward, approximately 25-35 cm [0.8 – 1.14 ft.] distance between them, the legs slightly bent according to the height of body build. The trunk slightly bent forward and the weight equally spread on both feet.

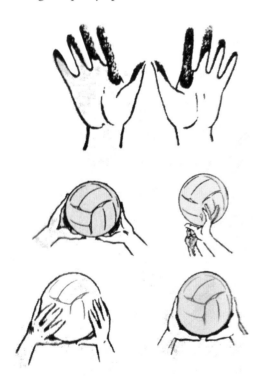

The hands on both sides of the trunk and the elbows bent. The palms open to take the shape of the ball; thumbs are lined up, at chin level, right next to each other at the same height in front of the face; the head looking forward.

The **middle positions** vary according to the knee angle and trunk inclination that depend on the performance requisites to deliver the ball to the hitter. The **defense position** is different than the low position in the distance between the two feet of 45-65 cm [1.47 – 2.13 ft.] and the position of the arms to the sides. This position is used for defending and receiving spikes, and it is very crucial to the progress and speed of the game. To receive the ball, the player's movement has to be balanced and fast so that the players can take the correct position to receive from above or below. In the last stage, hand and trunk position plays an important role in directing the ball.

Here are some drills to improve vision:

- Each player is given a ball to toss it in the air without making contact with another player.

- On one side of the court, a ball is given to 6 players moving in an irregular way. Each player has to choose a specific zone from 1 to 6. The ball is then set from zone 1 to 2 then to 3 onwards; each player has to look at the next one receiving the ball.

Here are some setting drills:

- Standing 2-3 m [6.5 – 9.8 ft.] away from the wall and throwing the ball against it at 3-4 m [9.8 – 13.1 ft.] height. The coach observes the players' movement and position of the trunk, hands, legs and feet.

- Two players standing at 5-7 m [16.4 – 22.9 ft.] distance from each other set the ball forwards and backwards. The set should be made specifically to the opposite player.

Picture 20-1

The receiving player has to take the correct position before setting the ball, by bending the knees and making sure that the ball is set overhead. (Picture 20-1)

- Setting the ball in a three-dimensional way between three or more players standing at 5-7 m [16.4 – 22.9 ft.] distance from each other. Each player has to move towards the ball during the set. (Picture 20-2)

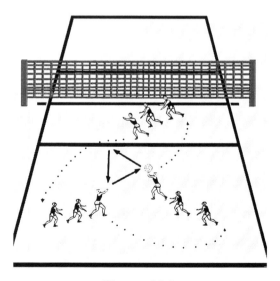

Picture 20-2

- Players stand in two lines facing each other with a distance of 5-7 m [16.4 – 22.9 ft.] between them. They have to focus on their position. Once the ball is set, each player goes back to the end of the line. (Picture 20-3)

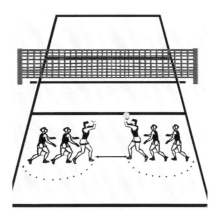

Picture 20-3

- The coach stands at the net and tosses the ball at 2-3 m [6.5 – 9.8 ft.] to zone 1 or 6 or in between. The player has to move forward to receive the ball and set back to the coach in zone 3. When the player moves towards the ball, the player should take the correct position and paying attention to the hands, feet and trunk. (Picture 20-4)

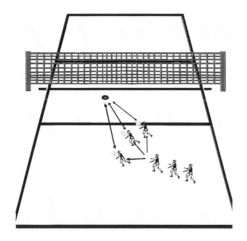

Picture 20-4

- Tossing the ball from zone 6 to zone 3 and then setting to zone 2 or 4 and from these zones back to zone 6. Setting the ball to zone 3 has to be at 1-2 m [3.2 – 6.5 ft.] from the net. Player of zone 3 has to face zone 4 or 2. The Setting in zone 2 or 4 takes place by tossing the ball 2-3 m [6.5 – 9.8 ft.] high to the edge of the net where the attacker is standing. (Picture 20-5)

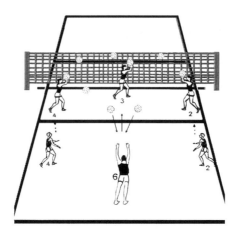

Picture 20-5

Drills to improve setting to specific zones:

- Player no. 1 has to toss the ball to the player facing him then rolls backwards, forwards or sideways. The opposite player receives the ball, tosses it back and performs another movement.

- Players are distributed in zones 4 and 2 on the attack line, one player in zone 3 by the net and one player in the center of the court no. 1 and the fifth player on the opposite side of the court to block. Player no.1 tosses the ball to zone 3 and from there the ball is set to zone 4 or 2 depending on the blocker's movement. If the blocker moves to the right then the ball is set to player no. 2 who sets the ball to player no. 1. If the blocker moves to the left then the ball is set from zone 3 to zone 4 and then direct it to player no.1. (Picture 20-6)

Picture 20-6

• The players stand in a square shape, in zones 1, 5, 2 and 4. The ball is directed from zone 1 to 4 and then to zone 2 followed by zone 5 and back to zone 1. The players move in the direction of the ball.

• A player stands in the center of the defense line facing the net, with other players in zones 2 and 4 and one standing in the opposite side of the court with the attack line. The player on the opposite side tosses the ball to the player standing in the center of the defense line, who directs it to zone 2 or 4, where these players direct it to the opposite side and move back to the end of the line. (Picture 20-7)

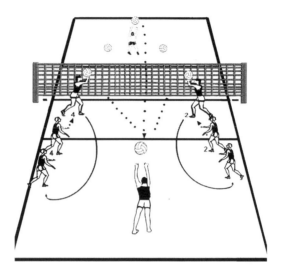

Picture 20-7

Besides these drills, players should practice by tossing the ball to specific zones for the attack, which is a crucial skill when it comes to executing strategies. When the team is composed of highly fit players and is constantly repeating and practicing tactics during training, then receiving the ball and directing it to the setter becomes an easy task.

It then becomes the setter's responsibility to think quickly who to set the ball to, in order to avoid a block from the opponent's team.

Chapter Twenty-One

RECEIVING

Receiving is performed by the player when receiving the ball from a serve, a set or a spike. When receiving, the hands are clasped together, the shoulders leaning forward, the arms extended and the ball is hit at the forearms. Sometimes, the player has to receive from a distance, in this case he has to be always facing the ball with the arms extended in that direction. In the case of a lateral ball the hands can't move vertically without directing them to receive the ball.

In order to master receiving and setting, the players have to previously decide to whom and where they should direct the ball. Receiving can be done with one hand as well by making a fist and fully extending the arm.

Here are some receiving drills:

- The player has to throw the ball against the wall and quickly move to receive it with his forearms while facing it.

- The ball is tossed to the players standing in zones 1-6-5, and each player has to receive the ball and redirect it to the coach in zone 3. (Picture 21-1)

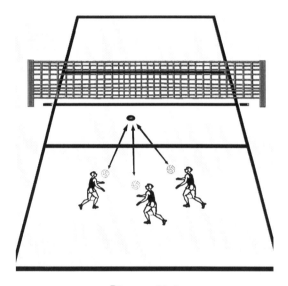

Picture 21-1

- The coach tosses the ball to each player and asks them to direct it to a specific zone.

- The coach tosses the ball directly at the net and the player has to receive it with one hand. The ball falling near the net has to be received close to the floor without touching the net.

The player that receives the ball falling off the net has to stand laterally so he will be able to hit it. It is important as well to receive the ball coming from the right side in the middle of the net with the right hand and the one coming from the left side with the left hand.

- Receiving the ball in one zone with one hand then with both hands. Whilst moving, the player tosses the ball in the air then receives it with the left hand, then with the right hand and finally with both hands.

- Receiving between players. Two players stand opposite each other and receive the ball with one hand or both hands while paying attention to their feet movement.

- Players face each other at 5-6 m [16.4 – 19.6 ft.] distance: one player near the net and the others facing him in a line deep in the court. The player standing by the net tosses the ball. The player facing him moves to receive the ball and returns back to the end of the line. (Picture 21-2)

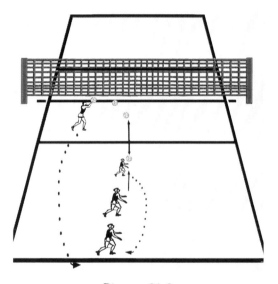

Picture 21-2

- One player serves the ball and the one standing on the opposite side of the court receives it and direct it to zone 2 or between zones 2 and 3. (Picture 21-3)

Picture 21-3

- The players have to receive a spike and redirect the ball to different places in the court according to the coach's instructions. (Picture 21-4)

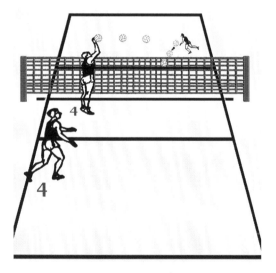

Picture 21-4

Chapter Twenty-Two

ATTACKING

Attacking or spiking is one of the most important skills in volleyball due to its effect and impact on the course of the game. It is executed with the palm of an open hand in a whipping movement from the wrist, while swinging the arm then jumping to hit the ball. The approach for the spike starts by the player positioning himself 2-4 m [6.5 – 13.1 ft.] from the net and taking the defense position to vertically jump and hit the ball. The player takes a 70-90 cm [2.2 – 2.9 ft.] step then places his body weight on both heels, bends the knees and swings the arms back like a pendulum, then forward and up while jumping.

The right arm is drawn back behind the head as the player rises so the open palm faces the sky, and then hammers the ball with the open right hand by snapping the wrist, swiveling the torso, pushing the metatarsi and extending the knees and pelvis.

The jump ends by placing the hitting hand behind the shoulder, the elbow forward and the trunk slightly arched. The ball is hit in its top third downward into the opponent's court.

After that, the player lands on both metatarsi by bending the knees to absorb the body weight and balancing to prevent falling over. (Picture 22-1)

Picture 22-1

Spiking isn't an easy strategy because the player has to move forward, jump, hit the ball and descend. The spiker depends on the setter and the agreed signals between them regarding the required strategy. Lately some teams started spiking by jumping on one foot as it gives them more speed to execute a certain strategy.

Here are some spiking drills:

- The setter stands in zone 3 and sets the ball to zone 4. The player in zone 4 spikes to zones 1-5-6 of the opposite side.

- The setter sets the ball from zone 2 to zone 3 and the player standing in this zone spikes to zones 5 and 6 of the opposite side.

- Setting the ball from zone 3 to zone 2 where the player spikes to zones 5-6-1 of the opposite side.

- Repeating the previous drill adding a block on the opposite side while correcting the hands and feet movement during the spike.

- A player serves to zone 1 where the ball has to be received and redirect it between zones 2 and 3. In the meantime, the setter has to move from the defense line to his place in order to set the ball either to zone 4 or 2 or 3 where the attackers have to spike to the defense line of the opposite side.

Choosing the right place to direct the spike shows a great deal of experience, tactical skill, knowledge of the opponents' capacities and coordination amongst players. The success of the spike depends on its strength and speed which makes it hard for the opponents to guess its direction. It depends as well on the spiker's personal view of the situation, the place where he stands and the approach he takes to spike. For example:

- Standing in zone 4 on the attack line around a meter [3.2 ft.] from the side line, the player gradually moves backwards to the left and then vertically forward to the net to spike from zone 4.

- A player stands in zone 2 far from the sideline and deep in the court towards the left and then moves back a little then forward to spike from zone 3 or 2.

- The player in zone 3 stands at 2m [6.5 ft.] from the net, avoids receive a serve in order to spike in zone 3.

- If the player in zone 3 wants to spike from zone 2 or 4 the player has to go back behind the 3 m [9.8 ft.] line to the right or the left from the center of the court i.e. around 2 m [6.5 ft.] away from the sideline without disturbing the other players.

- The spiker should mislead the blockers on the opponent's team.

- The spiker has to be ready at all times to spike.

- The spiker shouldn't disturb the interaction amongst the players on the team and should know what to do to in order to avoid a block from the opposite side.

Spiking in different ways: sometimes from a close set to the net and other times from a long set, in order to disturb the opponent's block. For example:

- Hitting the ball on the blockers fingertips so it changes direction or swerves out of court.

- Formally executing the strategy such as setting while jumping to spike.

- Thinking smartly when the ball is above the net between the attackers and the blockers.

- Spiking in different shapes, colors and sizes in order to ground the ball on the other team's court. The attacker executes a spike to the places indicated by the coach. This exercise can be made harder by shouting out the direction while the attacker is taking the first step to spike or is already in the air.

- The defenders move according to the ball hit by the attacker from the other side. In this case the attacker has to hit the ball at a specific defender.

While the ball is being received and directed to the setter, the attacker has to look at the other team's players and identify the way their defense is reacting, while the hitter takes the first step and before the ball is hit.

Attack drills:

- When spiking, the attackers in zones 2-3-4, have to direct the ball to zone 1 on the opposition's court or by a light hit to zone 5.

- The attacker in zone 4 spikes to zone 6 of the opposite side, during which the blockers in zones 2 and 3 of the opposite side perform a block.

- The attackers stand in one line in zones 3 and 2. On the opposite side the blockers stand in zones 4-3-2. The ball is set from zone 3 to zone 2, if the defenders block this ball and the attacker directs the ball to an empty spot on the opposite side.

When the ball is received by one of the players of the attack line then the two other players don't change places, they only move away from the net to prepare for the spike. The player executing the second set shouldn't leave the spot very quickly before identifying the flight path of the ball as well as its speed in order to choose the place and the right position to toss the ball to the hitter.

The results of the spike often depend on the second set, the way the ball is received and whether the reception was good and correct; then the strategy can be properly executed by setting the ball to the attacker who doesn't face a block from the other side. The setter has to be able to perform different kinds of sets such as snatch, high set, center and low as well as long sets from zone 2 to zone 4, setting from one zone to another or even in the same zone. The setter has to know where each player on the opponent's team stands, where a spike should be directed to and the approximate distance between him and the attacker.

One of the main setting characteristics is to set the ball from the edge of the net or the depth of the court to the exact zone that will benefit the team, i.e. where the spiker stands. If the ball reception was easy then the setter has to automatically set it to the zones close to the net.

Chapter Twenty-Three

BLOCKING

Blocking is a fundamental defensive skill used by the team to abort the attack of the opponent's team. Blocks can be done with one, two or three players. When blocking with two or three players, it is crucial that they control their steps in order to stand close to each other, time their jump and lift their arms and shoulders above the net to execute various forms of block depending on the direction of the spike. Blocks can be closed, half closed or open. A block is a defense tool that requires moving to the zone facing the attack to block by jumping and lifting the hands above the net.

It requires as well moving laterally alongside the net in successive steps, by lifting the open hands to chest level while moving and jumping as well as watching the attacker and the ball at all times, from the serve to the spike i.e. from the moment the ball is tossed by the setter.

Here are some blocking drills:

- The player stands on an elevated object so the ball can be held above the net. The player on the opposite side performs a block in zones 1, 2 or 3 by touching the ball with both palms.

One-person block

- Two players stand along the attack Line in zone 2 and 3. When the coach signals, they perform a block in zone 2 and then in zone 3.

Two-person block

- Two players stand near the net in zones 3 and 4. When the coach signals they perform a block in zone 3 and then in zone 4.

- Players stand in zones 2-3-4 on the court. The player in zone 3 moves towards the player in zone 4, and together they perform a block. When player of zone 3 returns to the place, the player repeats the same operation by moving to zone 2 to perform a block with the player of that zone. The focus in this drill should be on the speed of movement and the timing of jump.

- Players stand in zones 2-3-4. When the coach signals, they move to perform a collective block, first in zone 2 then in zone 3 and finally in zone 4. The operation is repeated in the opposite way.

Three-person block

PART SEVEN

DEFENSE STRATEGIES

Chapter Twenty-Four
TACTICAL DEFENSE STRATEGIES

There are three kinds of defense methods to prevent the ball from touching the ground in volleyball: blocking, protecting and setting.

Coaches have to previously organize different defense strategies in order to apply them during the training, so that each player knows how to move during the game, particularly when the ball is being received.

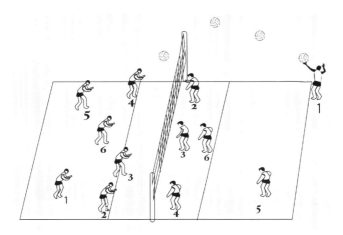

When the opponent's team serves, each player on the defending team has to watch the ball, take the necessary position to receive and closely watch the movement of the opponents. Depending on this evaluation, the defenders will choose where to set, block, receive a spike or protect the blockers and attackers.

Chapter Twenty-Five

BLOCKING STRATEGIES

Blocking is considered the first line of defense. The one player block is used when the tactical coordination of the opponent's team is difficult and fast, which means a blocker for each attacker.

There are two ways to block with one player: mobile and non-mobile. The mobile block is done from one specific side to abort the spike, by moving opposite to where the attacker is spiking.

Non mobile is when the defender blocks from his zone without moving. This type of blocks is used when the attacker spikes opposite the defender. The one player block requires choosing the right place to block, jump, lift the hands, and position the palms as well as how high to lift the hands above the net.

When spikes are repeated from middle or high sets, then the blocker has to time his jump after the attacker's and precisely when his hand gets near the ball to hit it. However, if the attacker is spiking from a snatch (low) or long set, then the blocker has to jump at the same time as the attacker. If the set for the spike is away from the net then the blocker can jump a bit later.

If attacking from the first set or the ball is thrown in an empty spot, then the blocker has to jump twice periodically in order to block. In these two cases, the blocker has to watch the attacker's movement and block at the last moment, in a way not to reveal where he will be blocking from. When blocking, all the players should be attentive to any precautionary sudden move. If the spike is close to the net, then the blocker has to empower his hands by bending them forward towards the ball. If the ball is 2 [6.5 ft.] to 3 m [9.8 ft.] far from the net, then the blocker has to lift both hands straight without bending the palms. On the other hand, if the spike is directed at a certain spot, then the blocker has to put his hands in front of the ball as if blocking in both directions. Blocking a spike coming from zone 4 or 2 should be done by curling the hands to block the ball.

When blocking a spike coming from zone 4 and directed to zones 1 and 2, then the blocker has to put his right palm tilted towards the right side of the ball's direction and the left palm straight. Before executing a spike, the blocker has to identify where the opponents will attack from, where does the strong attacker stand and how will he react to the ball set to him to spike. The second set gives the blocker a chance to figure out the attacker's movements on the opposite team.

Here are some blocking drills:

- Players stand in zones 2-3-4 and the same on the opposite side. One of the two sides attacks and the other side blocks, focusing on the hands movement.

- One player stands on the attack line, tosses the ball and hits it towards the opposite side or throws it to a certain spot and consequently the defender has to block it or protect it.

- One setter stands in zone 3, two attackers in zones 2 and 4, and the blockers on the other side. They will move according to the setter's movement who directs the second set to a specific spot and the defenders have to block the ball.

- The setter moves to zones 2 and 3, the attackers are in zones 3 and 4 and the blockers stand on the other side. Player of zone 3 spikes from a low set and player of zone 4 from a long or short set. When the setter moves, the blocker on the other side has to identify where the attack will take place by watching the attacker's steps in zone 3.

Chapter Twenty-Six

TACTICAL STRATEGY TO RECEIVE A SPIKE

The defender chooses the best place to receive the ball. If the direction of a spike is clear, then it will be easier for him to know where to receive from.

The defender has to estimate the direction of the spike, read the players on the opponent's team and know their capacities. When the set is far from the net, he shouldn't move forward to defend, but rather stays in the defense line to breach the gap in his team and coordinate with the rest of the players in order for the defense to be effective and coordinated.

The blocker should move without delay, be always attentive and quick to react at the right time to approach and jump lifting the trunk and hands high in the air.

Regardless whether blocking with one, two or three players, the team shouldn't rely only on it to defend. The rest of the players have to make the right movements in case the block is not successful by saving the ball before it touches the ground. Each player on the team has to be fully knowledgeable when it comes to his position and role in the defense strategy, in order not to disturb the teamwork during defense or protection or in both cases.

The defender has to stand where he thinks there is a big probability that the ball will fall. He has to pay attention as well to the attackers on his team so he can protect them by moving according to their movements.

The best guarantee for a successful defense is to know where the attacker on the opponent's team is spiking from, which makes it easy for the defending team to either block or protect.

Here are some defense drills:

- The players stand by the net in zones 4-3-2 and on the other side in zones 1-6-5.The players on the attack line have to toss the ball themselves and spike to the defense line, each to the player standing opposite. The defenders have to receive from above or below and direct the ball to specific zones. (Picture 26-1)

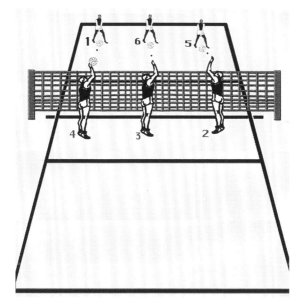

Picture 26-1

- The players stay in the same places as the previous exercise but the attackers have to direct the ball to different directions. Player of zone 4 hits to zone 6, player of zone 3 to zone 5 and player of zone 2 to zone 1. They can also hit to non-specific directions, as well as switch places on condition that the attacker doesn't defend and vice versa.

- The players stand as in the previous exercise but toss the ball and spike to the defense line or dip it to the attack zone for confusion. The defenders have to read the attackers and either stays in their zones or move forward to receive (in case of a dip).

- The setter stands in zone 3, two players in zones 4 and 2 and one player in zone 1 on the opposite side. The attacker in zone 4 and 2 spikes to zone 1 or dips to zone 2 on the other side. Player of zone 1 has to read the opponents in order to identify the attacker that will spike. (Picture 26-2)

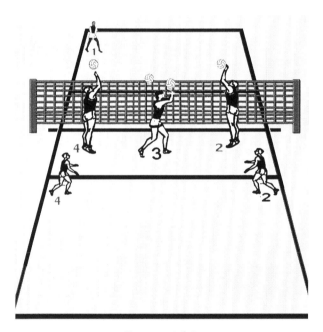

Picture 26-2

- Three players stand on the attack line in zones 2-3-4 and one player in zone 6 on the opposite side. The hitter in zone 4 spikes to zone 1, the hitter in zone 2 spikes to zone 5 and the defender has to automatically move to zones 1 and 5 to receive the spike. (Picture 26-3)

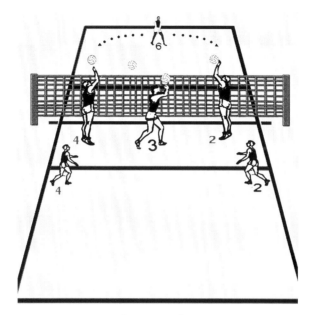

Picture 26-3

The blocker holds a key role in defense because he's responsible for defending and protecting at the same time. Meanwhile, the blockers in the collective block are divided to main blockers and secondary blockers.

When it comes to the collective block, the two players block is more used than the three players' one. Blocking with one player requires fast movement while the collective block requires coordination amongst the players.

Because of his technical and tactical level, the strong blocker who is the main organizer of the blocking operation always stands in the middle to block in zones 2 and 4. The blocking operation depends as well on the tactics and strategies of the opponent team. If the opponent team applies fast attack strategies, then the strong blocker has to block the ball to the edge of the net especially if the attacker is standing there.

Blockers have to be swift and able to read the attackers on the opponent's team especially those standing to the edge of the net. If the ball is spiked straight, then player of zone 3 has to block it. In all cases, main or skillful blockers are the ones responsible for blocking the ball during attack, while the others have to help and protect in the zone where the block is taking place, either in the middle or to the side.

On one hand, the fastest player with the most moves has to stand in the middle (zone 3). On the other hand, the approach taken by the blockers to execute a collective block depends on the ball, its direction at setting, the attack hit and its direction as well as the distance between the blockers. If the attack hit is directed at the blockers standing to the right, then the one to the left has to move to the right and vice versa. If the spike is directed between the blockers then they have to get closer to each other.

When blocking a direct hit, blockers have to have their palm curled and tense in the direction of the ball.

When blocking an attack hit from zone 4, the blocker moves from the center to the left where the ball is and places his hands at an angle to the net next to the other blocker's hand in order to block the ball. When blocking the attack hit in zone 2 blockers' hands alter automatically.

When blocking an attack hit in zone 4, the blocker moves to the opposite side slightly to the right and automatically curls his palms to block the ball, while the other blocker in the middle (zone 3) moves slightly to the left and puts his hands next to the other blocker's hands. A three player's block is done by players of zones 2 and 4 moving to the center to join the middle (zone 3) blocker. This kind of block is mostly used to block an attack hit in the center of the net.

Here are some of the possibilities that might happen during the games:

- If the attack hit is executed by the player of zone 2 or 3 on the opponent's team, then the blockers move to zone 3. The blocker in zone 2 stands between zone 2 and 3 to watch the attacker's movement in zone 4.

- If the blockers are getting ready to block with three players in the middle of the net, and the ball is set to the edge of the net at the last moment, then the blockers move fast from zones 2 and 3 or 3 and 4 to where the ball is being set.

When receiving an attack hit, only the collective cooperation gives positive results. The coordination has to take place amongst the defenders themselves, the defenders and the protectors, the defenders and the blockers, the protectors and the blockers and last but not least the protectors amongst each other's.

When choosing the right place to receive an attack hit, the defenders stand in unspecific places, where each player protects his zone and is ready at all time to help the others. The place choice is usually linked to the game situation and the number of defenders. The defenders coordinate amongst each other's in the defense line to execute the defense strategy.

The cooperation amongst the defenders defines the direction of the attack hit. Knowing the best place to occupy for maximum results depends on the players technical skills.

The cooperation amongst the defenders and the protectors is based on the agreed interaction, in specific situations, regarding where the protector stands and his zone, the number of protectors, where do the defenders stand and the coordination between defenders and protectors. The coordination between defenders and blockers takes different forms, for example: the blocker blocks a strong hit from the sideline, and as a result of that the defender slightly widens his zone in all possible directions to receive the ball.

Other times, after reading the attacker's movement, the defender coordinates with the blocker and makes a defense move. The protection's cooperation defines the blocking zone as well as the protector's spot and position. This cooperation depends on the game strategy applied by the defense in regards to the protectors' zone of interaction as well as the number of players filling this position.

Some situations can occur during the games that might require the attention of the coach and the necessary correction later in the training, for example:

- When performing a block with three players in the center of the net, the player in zone 6 participates in the protection by moving slightly from the defense line in case the attacker throws the ball behind the blockers. In this case, player of zone 1 moves forward as well as player of zone 5. (Picture 26–4)

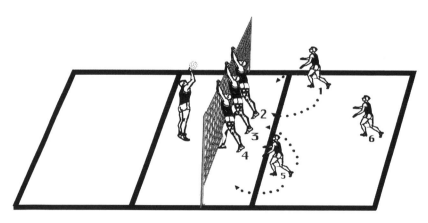

Picture 26-4

- When blocking with two players in zones 2 and 3, player of zone 6 moves to the attack line to protect the blockers from behind. The player that is not participating in the block i.e. the player in zone 4 has to protect in case the attacker throws the ball in his zone. The opposite is done if there is a two player block in zone 4, then the protection has to take place in zones 4 and 3 by the player in zone 5 moving behind the blockers. (Picture 26-5)

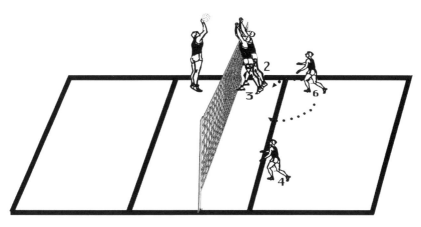

Picture 26-5

- When blocking with one player from any spot on the attack line, then the player in zone 6 has to protect with the help of the two players not participating in the block. (Picture 26-6)

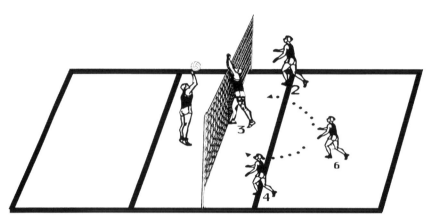

Picture 26-6

- The players in zones 2 and 3 block in zone 2 protected by the player in zone 4 who covers zone 2 and 3 in his protection. The player in zone 5 has to help protect zone 4. (Picture 26-7)

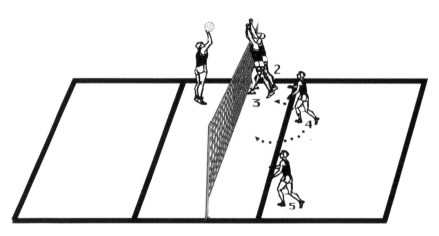

Picture 26-7

- The player in zone 1 protects when the two players in zones 2 and 3 are blocking the attack from zone 4 on the opposite side. In this case, the player in zone 4 helps protect by slightly moving backward – right.

When receiving the ball in different tactical ways, players have to show a wider range of cooperation whereby the weaker player has to be protected by the stronger ones, and the helper has to widen his zone of movement in order to be able to receive the ball without disturbing the attackers.

Since the ball can unexpectedly fall in any spot, players have to always be ready to receive even those standing on the attack line. When the player in zone 5 receives the ball, he has to move to the side of the court and the player in zone 1 has to be ready to protect, while players in zones 6 and 2 have to move as well to protect and direct the ball to the opposite side of the court.

Here are some cooperation drills:

- The two defenders of zones 1 and 5 participate in the protection process only when there is a two players block in zones 3 and 2, and the attack is coming from zone 4 on the opposite side.

In this case, the player in zone 1 moves closer, yet not too early, to the attack line to protect and takes the ready position at the last minute. This is the essence of cooperation inside the team. (Picture 26-8)

Picture 26-8

- When players in zones 4 and 3 are blocking in zone 4, the defender of zone 5 gets ready to protect by moving to the attack line. The defender in zone 1 gets ready to intervene as well in order to protect and help the player in zone 2.

- When three players are blocking in the center of the net i.e. players of zones 2-3-4, then the player in zone 6 has to move to the attack line to protect the blockers.

The players in zones 1 and 5 have to move closer to each other to protect or receive the ball. (Picture 26-9)

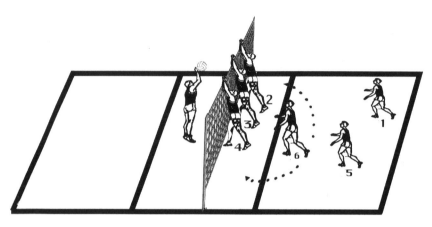

Picture 26-9

PART EIGHT

BEACH VOLLEYBALL

Chapter Twenty-Seven

HISTORY AND PROGRESS

Beach volleyball started on the beaches of Santa Monica, USA in the twenties. This sport didn't spread into Europe until recently, and it became internationally prominent in the late eighties. In 1996, it was included in the Olympic Games held in Atlanta, USA. The FIVB changed the dimensions of the beach volleyball court, making it smaller than the indoor one.

Dimensions of the whole court	Dimensions of court half
Old: 9 m x 18 m [29.7 ft. x 59.4 ft.]	Old: 9 m x 9 m [29.7 ft. x 29.7 ft.]
New: 8 m x 16 m [26.4 ft. x 52.5 ft.]	New: 8 m x 8 m [26.4 ft. x 26.4 ft.]

Beach volleyball, or sand volleyball, is a team sport played on sand. Two teams of two players separated by a high net, send the ball over the net in order to ground it on the opponent's court. The team has three touches for returning the ball.

Net's height varies according to categories and age.

Ages	Males	Females
17 years and above	2.43 m [8 ft.]	2.24 m [7.4 ft.]
16 and 15 years	2.24 m [7.4 ft.]	2.24 m [7.4 ft.]
14 and 13 years	2.12 m [7 ft.]	2.12 m [7 ft.]
12 years and below	2.00 m [6.6 ft.]	2.00 m [6.6 ft.]

Chapter Twenty-Eight

CERTAIN RULES FOR BEACH VOLLEYBALL

- The ball must be spherical, made of leather and rubber and water resistant. It can be of one color or more.

- Each team consists of two players. The coach is not allowed to participate during the championships organized by the FIVB. The team captain is the scorekeeper.

- Uniforms have to be practical and can come in different designs and colors. Players may wear a hat and sunglasses.

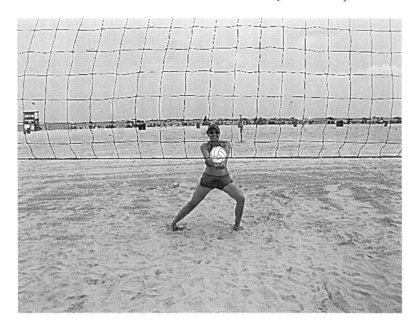

- Players may play barefoot or wear socks, or they can wear light comfortable shoes.

- They may not wear jewelry or other garments.

- Before the game, the referee asks the two team captains to toss a coin in order to choose either to serve or the side of the court to start the game. The game is played 2 sets out of 3.

- Substitution is not allowed.

- The rules of beach volleyball were established by FIVB and were first applied in 2002. Here are some of these rules:

  1. During one game, each team is allowed to have one time out of 30 second duration (two time outs were allowed before).

  2. In April of 2002, the FIVB agreed on changing the court's dimensions to 8 m x 16 m [26.4 ft. x 52.5 ft.] and to give one point to the team that wins the ball.

3. The winner of the game is the team that wins two sets out of three. If there is a tie break 1-1, then the game goes to 15 points. If the game is tied again at 15, then the first team to win the two-point advantage is the winner.

4. To win a set, the team has to reach 21 points with an advantage of 2 points at least (except in the third decisive set). In case of a tie at 20-20 the game is played until one team gains the two- point advantage (23-21, 22-20 etc.).

5. The players are allowed to move as they wish on their side of the court.

- Each team is allowed to touch the ball three times at the most before sending it into the opponent's court. Directional tipping is allowed as long as the player does not change the direction of the ball more than once.

In 2012 in Anaheim an addition has been commissioned by the 33rd FIVB world congress new rules of the game to be applied during the games between 2013 and 2016. Here are some of these modifications:

- During the match, only the captain is authorized to speak to the referees while the ball is out of play.

- Contact with the net by player is not a fault, unless it interferes with the play.

- A player of the serving team must not prevent an opponent, through individual screening, from seeing the server and the flight path of the ball.

By the 35th FIVB World Congress held in Buenos Aires, Argentina, the 2017-2020 official beach volleyball rules do not include any major changes to the current rules.

In the Rio Olympic Games 2016 in Brazil, the video challenge system helps to clearly see:

- the ball in or out

- block touch

- net fault

- antenna touch

- service foot fault

Summary

Players of any sport, whether individual or team sport, have to show sportsmanship and good ethics as well as positive attitude before, during and after the game. A competition normally takes place between two teams or two players depending on the nature of the sport, and as a result of that there is always a winner and a loser. Nevertheless, the main goal remains to play in a nice way that shows the player's skills, the team's capacities and the sport's and particularly volleyball's essence, whether technically or ethically. Once the nerves have calmed down, the coach of the losing team has to meet up with his players in order to go through the errors made during the game, give remarks without blaming anybody in particular for the loss and last but not least to positively encourage and motivate the players.

Afterwards, the coach needs to go through the remarks and suggestions in order to find solutions and avoid making the same mistakes in the future. He has to also prepare new strategies for the coming games. With the help of one of the assistant coaches, the coach has to provide each player on the team with an evaluation for his work and what he brings to the team before, during and after the games.

During the future games, the coaches have to keep their enthusiasm in order to motivate the players. They have to substitute certain players with others that are more ready and prepared, and always stress on winning till the last minute of the game.

Printed in Great Britain
by Amazon

72655912R00073